MARIGOLD

A One-act play

ROBERT SHEPPARD

Jasper Publishing

1 Broad Street Hemel Hempstead Herts HP2 5BW
Tel: 01442 263461 Fax: 01442 217102
jasperpublishing@ukbusiness.com
www.amdram.co.uk

MARIGOLD is fully protected by International Copyright Laws. All rights, including; Stage, Motion Picture, Radio, Television, Public Reading and Translation into Foreign Languages, are strictly reserved.

The sale of a script does not necessarily imply that the work is available for professional or amateur performance, and the holder of the copyright reserves the right to withhold permission to perform for whatever reason. If in doubt, please make application to the publisher.

To obtain information about acting fees payable on all professional and amateur performances of this work, together with any other details, please apply to the publisher;

Jasper Publishing
1 Broad Street Hemel Hempstead
Herts HP2 5BW
Tel: 01442 263461 Fax: 01442 217102

A licence must be obtained before any performance may be given, and all fees are payable in advance

ISBN 1 902837 15 0

British Library Cataloguing-in-Publication Data.
A catalogue record for this book is available from
The British Library.

MARIGOLD

CAST

Linda - Friend
Andrea - Sister
Elizabeth - Mother
Graham - Father
Simon - Brother
Miss Traynor - Teacher
Vicky - Friend
Jane - Fellow shop assistant

1.

The stage is dimly lit. A single spot comes up on Linda, downstage. During Linda's opening speech the other characters are barely seen.

Linda Dear Marigold: I don't really know what I want to say, or how to say it. I need to speak to you somehow, even though I know you'll never read this letter. But it's my only chance. They wouldn't let me see you. At the hospital. Something about family only, they said. I sort of understand what they meant - but we *were* like family, weren't we? Closer in lots of ways. Specially with your family. Oh, I know they're all right really - specially Simon - but you know what they say: you can choose your friends but not your family. Well, you chose me... and me you, of course. Remember, in infant school, how they put us next to each other on the first day. My mum said I cried like anything, but I don't remember. You didn't cry, Mum said.

Voice 1 Look at Marigold, Linda...

Linda Mum said she said.

Voice 1 ...she isn't crying. She's a big girl.

Linda And Mrs Murdoch always said you were the grown-up one in the class - I suppose that's why you always got those jobs like giving out the pencils and collecting the scissors.

Voice 2 There's never any missing when Marigold collects them.

Linda Mrs Murdoch used to say. It was like she was accusing all the rest of us of being secret scissor-snatchers or something. *(pause)* I wish they *had* let me see you. Then I could have said goodbye properly. Andrea said there wasn't much to see - you were all covered in bandages and tubes, she said.

Andrea It's no big deal, Linda...

Linda She said.

Andrea ..she's just lying there like a - a vegetable, or something.

Linda But then she's never been particularly sensitive, has she? Honestly, you'd never know she was your sister if you didn't... know. I've probably seen more of Andrea since the accident than in all the time before - even when we were all at school at the same time. But then I suppose older sisters never want much to do with you in public - bad for their image or something. And Andrea is certainly image-conscious, isn't she? I haven't got any brothers or sisters, so I don't really know... You were like a sister, sister and friend all at the same time. Now what am I going to do? *(her voice trails off. Pause)* I wish they had let me see you, Marigold.

2.

Hospital. Elizabeth, Graham, Andrea and Simon are in a group, physically close but emotionally distant from one another. There is a longish silence before anyone speaks.

Simon D'you think they'll let us see her again, Mum?

Andrea Why should they - there's nothing to see that we haven't seen already.

Simon I wasn't asking you. What do you care, anyway?

Elizabeth *(with extreme weariness)* I don't know, Simon. I'm sure they'll tell us if it's all right to...

Andrea I do care, of course I care.

Simon You've got a strange way of showing it. You've always been jealous of Marigold. And now she's...

Graham *(cutting in, sharply)* All right, Simon, that's enough.

Simon Well, it's true, Andrea's always...

Graham I said that's enough!

Silence.

Andrea *(quietly)* I can't help being jealous. I've always had to get on with things, never had much encouragement for anything...

Elizabeth Oh Andrea, how can you say that?

Andrea Quite easily, as a matter of fact. Marigold's always been your favourite, just because she's cleverer than me.

Elizabeth I've always tried to treat you all equally.

Andrea Well, you've not tried hard enough, as far as I'm concerned.

Graham Andrea, this is not the time...

Simon Andrea doesn't have much sense of timing.

Andrea *(not particularly forcefully)* Shut up, Simon.

Silence.

Elizabeth I know I might have done more for all of you. It's hard trying to balance things, sometimes. Your father's job takes him away a lot, so I've tried to make the right decisions when he's not been there.

Graham Someone's got to pay the mortgage.

Elizabeth I'm not criticising you, Graham. I'm just saying that it's been difficult, sometimes.

Graham You've never said so before.

Elizabeth Maybe I've never had the chance before. Or never taken the chance. It always seemed to be a case of getting round to things when there was time. Only there never seemed to be time, somehow. There was always so much to do just keeping things running smoothly - you know, the little things. Keeping the house respectable. Making sure everyone had clean clothes to wear. Feeding you all. It's difficult doing all that and having a job as well. But I never complained. I always thought it was... well, part of the job. I know that's what you think, Graham - a woman's place... and so on. I wish I'd been able to find time - make time - to talk to you all more often - at all, even - find out what you were thinking and feeling. All that time we were talking about Marigold's future I never once, really, talked, really talked, to her about it, found out what she really wanted. *(pause)* I've been much too busy to take notice of things. I've let your father have his own way too much, probably. It's easy to do that when you're tired.

Graham There's no point crying over spilt milk, Elizabeth.

Elizabeth Of course there's a point. If you don't, things will never change. You can't just carry on the same all the time. Especially when something like this has happened. It's too late now for me with Marigold -

Simon Don't say that, Mum. We don't know yet.

Elizabeth If we don't cry over spilt milk - if we can't change when things happen - we'll never learn. *(she pauses, on the verge of tears)* I'll never be able to know what Marigold felt... so don't say there's no point in crying, Graham... it's about all I can do now.

Silence

Graham All right, Elizabeth, you don't have the monopoly on feeling guilty. I know I should have made more time for you and the children. I thought I knew what was best for Marigold, that's all. Parents know these things, don't they? Learn from my mistakes, we're always telling them. But do they listen? Of course not. They always think they know best, don't they? I thought I knew best when it was time for me to leave school, but my father made me see the sense of leaving and getting a job. Earning's better than learning, he always said to me. And I haven't done badly, have I? I've provided for you all, kept a roof over your heads.

Andrea But you're never at home, Dad. We hardly see you. And when we do, it's just so you can tell us what we ought to be doing. Like me. I didn't get a choice, did I? No point in staying on at school, Andrea, you said. Go and get a job. Bring something in. Make yourself useful. Is that all you want for us - to make ourselves useful? Is that what you wanted for Marigold? Making her get that dead-end shop job so she could feel she was making herself useful?

Elizabeth Andrea, let's not -

Andrea Let's not what, Mum? Speak the truth?

Elizabeth Not now... not here...

Andrea What's wrong with here? If we weren't here we wouldn't be saying all this, would we? We'd just -

Simon Why can't you all just shut up? Marigold's in there, on the point of... just shut up, can't you? *(he rushes out, too upset to carry on)*

Andrea *(after a short pause)* Well, he's not the only one to have feelings. *(pause)* I always wanted to get on with Marigold. It's just that she always seemed to be the one who couldn't fail - even if her parents couldn't find time to talk to her. She was just so good at everything -

Elizabeth *(sharply)* What do you mean - was?

Andrea You know what I mean. It just didn't - doesn't - seem fair, somehow. I know I wasn't - I'm not - always very friendly to her. But she's my little sister - everyone knows sisters can't be friends until they're grown up. Sometimes not even then.

Simon enters and stands unseen by the others.

So I would have been - will be - when we are. Both of us. Grown up.

Graham We all need to make a fresh start.

Elizabeth Make more time.

Graham First thing we'll do when we're all home is just sit down and have a good chat.

Elizabeth Maybe we all need to get to know each other again.

Pause. After a few moments, Andrea notices Simon.

Andrea Simon?

Simon It's too late.

3.

Hospital. Linda and Vicky sit close together.

Vicky I don't know why they can't let us see her. It'd cheer her up if she saw her friends.

Linda I don't think she'd know we were there, Vicky. She's not conscious.

Vicky When she wakes up, then.

Linda She might not.

Vicky What - wake up? You mean she might...

Linda It was a bad accident.

Vicky Still, we're her friends. You'd think they might let us see her for a bit - just a minute or two - or at least let us know how she's doing.

Pause

What about that last rehearsal. Wasn't it a scream? I thought Miss Traynor was going to have a fit, it was so bad. Except Marigold, of course. She was perfect, as usual. When she did the sleep-walking scene I could feel all the hairs on the back of my neck go tingly. It was creepy. And then she drifts off moaning "To bed... to bed... to bed". And you just know she's not going to sleep, but die...

Linda gives her a sharp look.

Sorry - I didn't mean...

Linda I sometimes wonder what you've got in your head, Vicky. Is there *any* connection between your brain and your tongue?
Vicky Sorry. I didn't think.
Linda Precisely.
Vicky Sorry.

Jane approaches them, rather hesitantly.

Linda Hello.
Jane Hi. I was wondering - is this where Marigold...?
Linda Yes. She's in there.
Vicky But they won't let us see her.
Jane Oh.
Linda Do you know her?
Jane Sort of. I'm Jane.
Linda Oh, from the shop.
Jane Yes. Mr Porter said I ought to come.
Linda Mr Porter?
Jane The boss.
Linda Oh.

Silence

Jane How is she?
Vicky We don't know, really, they won't let us see her.
Jane Oh.
Linda She's in intensive care. We think she might... it's very bad.

Silence

Jane I didn't know her that well, really. She just worked in the shop Saturdays - you know. Busy day, Saturday, so we never had much of a chance to - you know. But she was doing really well.
Linda I don't think she enjoyed it very much.

Vicky My dad won't let me get a Saturday job. Says I need to spend all my time on schoolwork. Says if I don't I won't be able to get any job when I leave school, let alone in a shop.

Jane It's not that bad. It's not just serving, you know. You can be a management trainee.

Vicky Are you?

Jane No. *(pause)* Didn't fancy it. Could've been - you know. Just didn't fancy it.

Vicky I'd quite fancy that. That management thing. You get to tell everyone else what to do and that. That'd suit me all right. Only my dad says -

Linda Vicky, do you really think this is the time for discussing your career prospects?

Vicky Well, I...

Linda No. The answer is no.

Jane I'm not bothered about a career, really. Marigold could have had one - Mr Porter was quite keen on her, you know - as a trainee, I mean.

Linda She wasn't - isn't - interested. She could have done anything she wants. She was going to be so... is going to be... oh, God - it's just not fair!

She exits quickly, on the point of tears. The others remain, not looking at each other.

4.

Andrea and Simon are at home. There is an air of uneasiness.

Simon When are you going to the hospital?

Andrea I don't know.

Simon You could go now. Mum and Dad are there.

Andrea Simon, I've just got in. I'll go when I'm ready, all right.

Simon It was a bad accident.

Andrea I know it was bad. But me being at the hospital isn't going to change that, is it? *(pause)* Anyway, why aren't you there?

Simon I wanted to go. Dad thought it'd be better if I stayed here. I think he thinks I wouldn't be able to cope, or something. Honestly, he treats me as if I was still a kid.

Andrea You are still a kid.

Simon I'm nearly sixteen.

Andrea I rest my case.

Pause.

Simon At least I care - I'd be there if they'd let me.

Andrea I do care. I'm tired, that's all.

Simon You don't care. You never have as far as Marigold's concerned. You've always gone out of your way to be nasty to her, just because she can do things you can't. Why can't you just accept her for who she is?

Andrea She's my sister - there's not much I can do about it.

Simon What's that supposed to mean?

Andrea We just have to put up with each other, don't we? Just like I'm having to put up with you now.

Simon You don't have to put up with me. You could go to the hospital.

Andrea For heavens' sake, Simon, stop going on. I'll go when I'm ready.

Simon And suppose that's too late?

Pause.

Andrea What do you mean - too late?

Simon You know what I mean - like I said, it was a bad accident.

Silence.

Andrea You always have to do the 'right' thing, don't you? Just so that everyone can say how Simon is such a nice person. Especially Marigold. You've always wanted Marigold to like you more than me, haven't you? Why does it matter what she thinks? Why do you always go crawling to her when you want someone to say how wonderful you are?

Simon She's always been ready to listen. Not like you - or Mum and Dad.

Andrea You need to stand on your own two feet a bit more, Simon. You can't always rely on someone else to tell you what to do. *(pause)* Anyway - I could tell you what you want to hear just as easily as Marigold or anyone else. It's just that I'm more honest - you might not like what you get from me.

Simon No one likes what they get from you, Andrea.

She looks at him coldly for a few moments and then leaves.

5.

School. Linda and Vicky are talking to Miss Traynor, their English teacher.

Vicky What do you think will happen now, Miss? About the play?

Miss Traynor You mean because of Marigold, Vicky, is that it?

Vicky Well, yes.

Miss Traynor I don't think we should make any hasty decisions, do you?

Vicky Well, no. I just thought that if Marigold wasn't able to... you know.

Linda We don't know yet whether she'll be able to carry on or not, Vicky, do we? There's still thirteen weeks to go.

Miss Traynor Until we hear more about how she is, I don't want to make any changes.

Vicky It's going to be difficult rehearsing without her, though, isn't it? Lady Macbeth is quite an important character, isn't she?

Linda Of course she's an important character. That's why Marigold is playing the part - because she's better than anyone else.

Vicky Well, I wouldn't have played it the same as her. I think she's making her much too passionate - I'd be much colder.

Linda But you're not playing the part, are you?

Miss Traynor I don't think this is very helpful. The point is, although Lady Macbeth is an important part, there are lots of scenes she doesn't appear in, so we can re-schedule some of the rehearsals and then pick up on Marigold's scenes again when she's back.

Vicky We don't know when she'll be back, though, do we. Simon - her brother - says they think it was quite bad.

Miss Traynor Let's wait until we get some official news, Vicky, shall we? I don't want to replace Marigold if there's a chance she can carry on. I know I can rely on her to work at the part even harder if she's had to miss some rehearsals.

Linda Anyway, Miss Traynor, we haven't got anyone who could take over, have we?

Vicky gives her a hurt look.

I think the best thing would be - if Marigold is too ill to carry on - to cancel the play now and put it on again when she's better.

Vicky We don't know if she's going to get better. I could learn the lines ever so quickly, Miss. I know a lot of them already.

Miss Traynor *(gently)* Let's wait and see, Vicky, shall we?

Linda Yes - let's wait and see.

6.

Linda's letter.

Linda We've cancelled the play. We all thought it was best, even though Vicky - the daft bird-brain - thought you'd've wanted us to carry on. She kept going on about 'the spirit of the theatre' or something. I don't know where she gets it all from. She reads magazine articles and stuff she doesn't understand and then spills it all out to impress us. Who does she think she's fooling? Anyway, Miss Traynor and the rest of us felt we couldn't carry on. And then Vicky goes on about...

Vicky 'The curse of the Scottish play'!

Linda She's got about as much sensitivity as serving a pork chop at a barmitzvah! I know she's harmless, really - you can't help smiling a bit while you're beating her up!

Pause.

We had some good laughs, though, didn't we? What about that time we skived off to get your mum a birthday present in Woolworths? I'd never have dared if you hadn't made me. Do you remember how I wouldn't go to the local one and we had to catch the bus to Stanton to go to the one there so that no one would recognise us? And then we bumped into Miss Traynor by the pick'n'mix. Well, I didn't know it was her afternoon off and she lived in Stanton, did I? She would've blamed me as well if you hadn't owned up. You lost a few Brownie points there, Marigold. *(pause)* Still, it didn't take you long to get them back again - especially with Miss Traynor. Talk about 'do no wrong'. Funny how people have short memories when it suits them.

Pause.

That's all we've got, though, now, isn't it? Memories. They say your memory fades as you get older. Mine won't, Marigold. It won't.

7.

School. Linda and Vicky are waiting for Marigold to go to a rehearsal.

Vicky I can't get the hang of my character at all. I mean, there's not much to go on, is there? Third Witch. What does that tell you? They're all the same, aren't they? But Miss Traynor says we've got to make them different somehow. Maybe we should all have a different sort of nose or something. I was reading this article about Laurence Olivier and how he used to find his character through the make-up.

Linda Don't you think that's a bit of an exaggeration, Vicky?

Vicky No, not at all. This article said he often couldn't find the... *(trying to remember)* ...the kernel of his characterisation until he'd put on the make-up and looked at himself for hours and hours in a mirror. *(pause)* Even if he wasn't *playing* a colonel, apparently.

Linda So you're going to lock yourself in the bathroom with a false nose, are you?

Vicky Don't be daft. No one'd be able to go to the loo. *(pause)* No, I'll do it in my bedroom.

Linda I think you should just let the words do it for you. It's all there if you just look for it.

Vicky You sound like Marigold. Use the text, she says. It's all right for her. She's got some decent text to use. *(pause).* Where is she, anyway? We're going to be late if she doesn't get a move on.

Linda Perhaps she's in the loo getting into character!

Vicky No - I've just been in there - she's not... oh, shut up, you!

Pause.

Linda *(with slight concern)* It's not like Marigold to be late, though. 'Specially for a rehearsal. *(pause)* Anyway, what are you talking about? You've got some decent lines, haven't you?

Vicky Yeah, right! Like "A drum! A drum! Macbeth doth come!" Real deep stuff! I'd fancy doing Lady M., so long as I didn't have to do the - you know - the rude bits!

Linda I don't know what you're talking about, Vicky.

Vicky Come on, Lind. The *rude* bits! "Come to my woman's... - you know. And "I have given..."

Linda What?

Vicky You know. *(she mouths)* Suck... I just couldn't say things like that without curling up. I don't know how Marigold does it with such a straight face.

Linda Maybe it's something to do with being talented. *(pause)* Then again, perhaps she's just spent plenty of time locked in the bathroom!

Vicky You don't give up, do you?

Andrea approaches them.

Hi, Andrea. How's things?

Andrea Are you waiting for Marigold?

Linda Yes. She's a bit late. Do you want us to give her a message, or something?

Andrea No. I've got a message for you. She's not coming. *(awkward pause)* There's been... an accident.

Vicky What - you mean the bathroom door's stuck!

She giggles rather stupidly - Linda gives her a sharp look.

Linda What sort of accident?

Andrea It's Marigold - she's been - hurt.

Linda Hurt?

Andrea They've taken her to hospital.

8.

Home. Simon is doing his homework. Elizabeth is arranging flowers.

Simon Mum -

Elizabeth Yes?

Simon Did you do Tudor history at school?

Elizabeth I can't remember, Simon.

Simon I can't see the point, really.

Elizabeth The point of what?

Simon I mean, it's quite interesting, I suppose... but it's not really relevant, is it?

Elizabeth What isn't, dear?

Simon looks at her and shrugs, giving up.

Simon Has Marigold spoken to you about going to university?

Elizabeth About what, dear?

Simon Going to university.

Elizabeth stops what she is doing and looks at him.

Elizabeth No, she hasn't. *(pause)* Should she have done?
Simon She wants to. Miss Traynor's been talking to her about it.
Elizabeth She's not said anything. Anyway, I don't really know about things like that. She'll have to talk to your father about it.
Simon *(under his breath)* Fat lot of good that'd do.
Elizabeth What?
Simon You know what he thinks - it's all a waste of time.
Elizabeth Well, he knows best about these things. He's had a lot of experience.
Simon Not of university.
Elizabeth That's not done him any harm. *(pause)* Look, Simon, I really can't talk about this. Marigold will have to speak to your father about it when they get in.
Simon You could at least have a chat to her about it. I know she wants to. She'd like to feel you're at least taking an interest. You always leave everything to Dad. Why can't you have a say?
Elizabeth All right, Simon. I'll talk to Marigold when she gets home. Get on with your geography.
Simon History.

Silence. Andrea comes in, not in a good mood.

Andrea If I have to deal with another 'no claims bonus' this century I'm going to scream. Honestly, you'd think people would know that 'no claims' means what it says, wouldn't you? But apparently not! "It was only a little claim", they say - "why can't I have the bonus?" Are people stupid, or what?
Simon Good day, then, was it?

Andrea glares at him.

Elizabeth Andrea didn't go to university, did you?
Andrea *(with some feeling)* No, Mum, I didn't.
Elizabeth She hasn't done badly.
Andrea Mum! Are you living on the same planet as the rest of us?
Elizabeth Andrea, don't -
Andrea I come home every day worn out from working in a dead-end job in a last-resort office with no-hope people and you say I haven't done badly. Do you take any notice of what your family are doing or feeling?
Elizabeth Andrea, there's no need to...
Andrea Go out and get a job, Andrea, you said, it doesn't matter what.
Elizabeth Well, your father -
Andrea Earn a wage, you said, you don't want to waste another three years being educated about things that won't do you any good.
Elizabeth Your father thinks -

Andrea We all know what he thinks. We've heard it often enough. But have you ever stopped to wonder if what he thinks is actually right?

Silence. The doorbell rings.

Simon I'll get it.

He exits.

Elizabeth All right, Andrea. I realise you've had a bad day...
Andrea I've always had a bad day. Not that you care.

Simon returns with Linda.

Elizabeth *(with a sense of relief for the opportunity of changing the subject)* Hello, Linda. How are you?
Linda Hello. Hi, Andrea. Is Marigold here? We've got a rehearsal.
Elizabeth She's not home yet, Linda. She was popping into the shop on her way home to collect her wages. She oughtn't to be long.

Linda senses the atmosphere. There is an awkward silence.

How's the play going?
Simon You never ask Marigold that.
Linda *(pleased to be able to break the silence)* It's going really well. Miss Traynor's quite pleased.
Elizabeth What are you playing?
Linda I'm the stage manager.
Elizabeth Oh, that's nice, dear.
Linda Most important job, they keep telling me.

Pause.

Simon How's Marigold getting on?
Andrea *(with a hint of sarcasm)* Brilliant as usual, I suppose.
Linda *(after a momentary pause)* She's doing it fantastically, actually. Really good. Every time she's on the whole thing sort of comes to life.
Andrea *(even more sarcastic)* How wonderful!
Elizabeth I was nearly in a production of *Hamlet* myself when I was at school.
Simon It's *Macbeth*, Mother.
Elizabeth Oh yes, that's right. I remember Marigold telling me she'd got a good part.
Simon She's playing Lady Macbeth - I suppose that's quite a good part, as parts go.

Linda She's got into the character really well. Honestly, she makes my flesh creep some of the time, the way she says the lines. The sleepwalking scene makes your spine tingle!

Simon Are you going to see it, Mum?

Elizabeth Oh, well, I'll have to speak to your father. When's it on?

Linda At the end of term, in about two and a half months.

Elizabeth We'll have to look in the diary, then.

Simon I'm coming, Linda. What about you, Andrea?

Andrea What?

Simon Are you going to see Marigold's play?

Andrea Don't know. Might do. Shakespeare doesn't do much for me, really.

Simon I'm coming, anyway.

Silence for a few moments.

Elizabeth She ought to be here by now. I can't think what's keeping her.

Pause; then, for the sake of making conversation...

It must be a lot of work for Miss...

Linda Traynor. Yes - that's what she's always saying. Says we don't appreciate it.

Andrea But of course you all do - especially Marigold, I expect.

Linda *(quietly, not rising to Andrea's tone)* Marigold knows what it takes, yes.

Pause.

Look, I'd better go. I'm supposed to be setting up for the rehearsal. Perhaps Marigold's gone straight there. She's probably fuming by now because nothing's ready. *(pause)* I'll see myself out.

She goes.

Elizabeth I don't know why you didn't take part in things like that when you were at school, Andrea.

Andrea Maybe because I didn't want to.

Elizabeth But I'm sure you would have enjoyed it. Marigold seems to get so much out of it.

Andrea Marigold. Marigold. It's always Marigold, isn't it. Why can't you just accept the fact that I'm not Marigold, Mother. In case you've forgotten, my name is Andrea.

Elizabeth Don't be silly, dear, of course -

The doorbell rings. Nobody moves.

Simon *(after a few moments)* I'll get it, shall I?

He exits. There is a silence.

Elizabeth Andrea, I don't think...

Andrea glares at her. Silence. Simon returns.

Simon Mum, there's a couple of police officers at the door. *(pause)* They say can they speak to you.

9.

Shop. Graham is buying an evening paper and is served by Jane.

Graham Evening Standard, please.
Jane Evening Standard? Thirty-five pence, please.

He gives her some money.

Jane *(as she gives Graham his change)* You're Marigold's dad, aren't you?
Graham Yes, I am. How did you know?
Jane I've seen you sometimes on Saturdays when you've dropped her off.
Graham Ah, I see. *(pause)* How's she getting on?
Jane *(not especially interested)* Quite well, I think. Mr Porter - the boss - seems pleased. The customers seem to like her - well, she's friendly, isn't she?
Graham Yes - yes, I suppose she is. I've never really thought about it. *(pause)* So she's doing well, then?
Jane Yeah. Mr Porter wants her to come and work here full-time when she leaves school. Management trainee, he says.
Graham Does he, indeed?
Jane Yeah. In fact, I heard him the other day trying to persuade her to leave school now -
Graham What - before she's taken her A-levels?
Jane Yeah, something like that. He says she could do a lot worse.
Graham He could be right. What did Marigold say?
Jane She wasn't keen, really. Actually, tell you the truth, she's not that keen on the job at all. She wants to go to university or something, doesn't she?
Graham Yes, maybe - I haven't had a chance to talk to her about that.
Jane That's what she told me, anyway.
Graham Well, thanks, er...
Jane Jane.
Graham Yes, thanks, Jane. That's good news about Marigold. *(pause)* Well, 'bye for now.
Jane 'Bye.

10.

Andrea and Simon are sitting at home, ignoring each other. After a few moments, Elizabeth comes in.

Elizabeth Well, it's all go in here and no mistake.

Pause.

I do wish you two would be quiet for a moment and let someone else get a word in.

Andrea gives Elizabeth a 'ha-ha very funny' sort of look.

Simon Andrea's had a bad day at work.
Andrea I haven't said that.
Simon You didn't have to. Anyway, do you ever have a good day?
Andrea Actually, today wasn't too bad, as a matter of fact.
Elizabeth Oh good, Andrea. I'm sure your father will be pleased to hear that.
Graham *(entering as Elizabeth is speaking)* Pleased to hear what?
Elizabeth Andrea's had a good day at work, she says.
Andrea I didn't say it was good - I said it wasn't too bad. There's a difference.
Graham Anyway, at least you can appreciate the value of having a job. Doing something useful and earning a bit of money instead of wasting your time.
Simon Wasting your time doing what, Dad?
Graham You know what I mean, Simon. Wasting your time at the taxpayers' expense on getting a lot of so-called 'knowledge' that isn't going to get you a better job anyway, at the end of the day.
Simon *(under his breath)* Here we go!
Elizabeth Graham - I've been meaning to speak to you. Marigold's been on at me again.
Graham Oh yes?
Elizabeth You know she's really keen to do well at school.
Simon She is doing well, isn't she?
Andrea Don't we take it as read that Marigold does well at everything?
Elizabeth Well, you know what her teacher said last week, Graham. And Marigold is very keen to go to university.
Andrea I might have been keen to go to university, but a fat lot of good it did me.
Simon Don't talk daft, Andrea. You couldn't wait to get out of education. We didn't see you for dust at the end of your last term. Miss Traynor said it was like watching Road Runner disappearing over the horizon!
Andrea I suppose you think that's funny.
Simon *(after a moment's reflection)* Yeah, actually I do.
Graham You were sensible, Andrea. You recognised the value of getting a decent job and -
Andrea Getting a job, anyway.

Graham Well, you have to start somewhere. You can't expect to be spoon-fed. I wasn't.

Short pause.

Elizabeth It's just that Marigold seems to be the right sort to - you know... She's getting good grades in nearly everything and it seems a shame if she can't at least try. It seems logical, somehow.

Graham You mean go to university just for the sake of going? With no idea what you're going to do when you've finished. There's just no point, Elizabeth. I've done all right without wasting three or four years of my life, and Andrea's doing all right.

Andrea Depends what you mean by 'all right'.

Simon You didn't want to go, anyway.

Andrea That's not the point. I should have been given the choice.

Elizabeth Well, what's best for you isn't necessarily what's best for Marigold, is it? I mean, she's different.

Andrea *(exploding)* And don't we all just know it! Marigold this, Marigold that, look at wonderful little sister Marigold, isn't she doing well? Could she ever do anything wrong as far as you're concerned?

Elizabeth Andrea, I didn't mean -

Andrea I'm going out! And the sooner I can find somewhere else to live, the better!

She storms out. There is a heavy silence.

Simon Don't you think it would be a good idea to involve Marigold in this? It's hardly fair to be discussing her future when she's not even here to speak for herself.

Graham Where is she, anyway?

Elizabeth At a rehearsal for that play.

Simon She's only playing the lead in *that* play.

Graham She can have her say if she likes. No one can accuse me of not listening to others. *(pause)* Where did you say she is?

Elizabeth Well, you talk to her then, Graham. You tell her why she can't go to university.

Simon And then you can tell me why I can't go.

Graham All right, Elizabeth. I'll have a chat with her when she gets home. I'm sure she'll be able to see my point of view. She's a reasonable girl, after all. *(pause)* Must get that from my side of the family.

11.

Linda's letter.

Linda I wish your parents had had the chance to see you in the play, Marigold. I don't think they have any idea how good you were going to be. Even Andrea would have been impressed, although she wouldn't have admitted it, of course. Simon knows it was going to be something special. You probably weren't aware - being in it, you know - that he used to sneak in at the back of the hall to watch. He asked me not to tell you - thought it might distract you or something. Maybe if your parents had seen you do something like that their feelings about you would have changed. I don't mean they didn't - don't - love you. It just seemed to me that they never, somehow, showed it very much. I know you felt that, sometimes, even though you didn't let it get to you. Why is it always when it's too late that we wished we'd told people what we really feel? *(pause)* Did I? I wonder. Do you know how much I'm going to miss you? I'll never have another friend like you, Marigold - never.

12.

School. Miss Traynor has asked Elizabeth and Graham to come and see her about Marigold.

Miss Traynor She really does stand every chance of getting to a really good university. She's such a conscientious student, you see. And very talented too, of course.
Elizabeth Well, we've always known she was bright, haven't we, dear?
Graham Bright, yes. But that doesn't automatically mean she should go to university, does it? It's not right for everyone, you know.
Miss Traynor No, of course, you're quite right, Mr Simmons. But in Marigold's case, I do feel...
Elizabeth It's what she wants, isn't it?
Graham Is it? She's never said so to me.
Elizabeth Well, dear, she doesn't often get the chance to talk things over with you, what with you being away so much. *(slight pause)* And...
Graham And...?
Elizabeth Well, I think she feels that she wouldn't get a very sympathetic hearing.
Graham What makes you say that?
Elizabeth You don't allow much room for... negotiation, sometimes.
Graham Look, Elizabeth, I-
Miss Traynor Obviously it's important that you think Marigold makes the right choices. But I do think we must be careful not to disregard what she wants.

Pause.

Graham Well, everybody knows how I feel about it.

Elizabeth Yes, dear. Everybody knows.

13.

Simon and Jane, meeting.

Jane Simon.
Simon Oh, hi.
Jane Your sister - I think she's coming to work in our shop, isn't she?
Simon Oh, yeah. Dad sort of... persuaded her that it would be a good idea. She's not particularly keen, though.
Jane Tell her it's all right, really. Saturdays are always busy so you never have time to stop and think too hard about what you're doing there. I don't, anyway.
Simon Marigold'd much rather be doing her homework or learning lines for the play or something. She's always been like that. But Dad says she needs some 'training for life', as he puts it. He doesn't seem to understand that not everyone is going to live the same kind of life he has. Thank God!
Jane P'raps he'll change when he realises Marigold doesn't want to do it.
Simon Him? Never. He doesn't see change as an option for himself. Others are the ones who have to change, not him.

Pause.

Jane Well, tell Marigold it's not as bad as all that. *(pause)* All right - it is as bad as all that... whatever all that is. But it can be a laugh sometimes. You know, occasionally. *(pause)* She'll be okay.

Pause.

Simon Right. I'll tell her.

14.

School. Linda is talking to Miss Traynor.

Linda Marigold's really pleased about getting Lady Macbeth, Miss.
Miss Traynor Well, that was an easy decision to make. There was no one else who came close, really.
Linda Vicky was quite disappointed not to get the part. But I think she'll be more... effective as a witch.
Miss Traynor Yes. Vicky will be fine as a witch.

Pause.

Linda I just hope Marigold will be able to cope - at home, I mean.
Miss Traynor What do you mean?

Linda Well, her mum and dad - they're not really into plays and things. Her dad wants her to get a job.

Miss Traynor I'm sure Marigold will be able to cope, Linda. If she wants to get a job I'm sure she's weighed up all the pros and cons.

Linda But I don't think she does really want a job. Her dad can be a bit pushy about that sort of thing. He thinks it's more important than school, somehow.

Miss Traynor Well, Marigold's sensible enough to know what's right for her. She's very talented - at all sorts of things. I'm sure you know that, as her friend.

Linda Yes, of course.

Miss Traynor Right then. You don't need me to interfere, do you? *(pause)* Now... about tomorrow's rehearsal. We're doing the sleepwalking scene first. Can you make sure the stage is clear so that we can start on time?

Linda Yes, Miss Traynor. It'll be ready.

15.

Vicky and Jane.

Vicky You work at that shop, don't you?

Jane Which shop?

Vicky The one you work at.

Jane Well, obviously. So what?

Vicky My friend may be coming to work there.

Jane Oh yeah. Who's that then?

Vicky Marigold Simmons.

Jane Don't think I know her.

Vicky Of course, she might not.

Jane Might not what?

Vicky Come and work at your shop.

Jane It's not my shop.

Vicky You know what I mean.

Pause

Jane Well, is she or isn't she?

Vicky What?

Jane Coming to work at the shop.

Vicky I don't know. She might.

Jane You said that already.

Vicky She might not because she's into - you know - school - and that.

Jane *(barely interested)* Oh.

Vicky And she's probably going to be in the play.

Jane What's that, then?

Vicky Macbeth.

Jane Macbeth. *(pause)* Is that the one with the fairies?

Vicky Witches.

Jane Oh yeah. *(pause)* So she's not really interested, then.
Vicky In the play?
Jane In working in the shop.
Vicky Oh. Doesn't seem to be. Of course, I reckon I know why.
Jane Why's that, then?
Vicky It's because of the deep-rooted turmoil in her family that just bubbles away beneath the surface. She's not sure of herself, see. Not sure what she wants. I was reading this book by this Austrian bloke - Frood or something. He reckons our whole life is just a dream.
Jane A dream?
Vicky Yeah.
Jane You mean like if we pinch ourselves we won't exist any more? Do me a favour.

She starts to exit.

Vicky *(following her off)* That's what it said in this book. Of course, I haven't got to the end yet.
Jane You mean you haven't woken up yet.
Vicky Yes - something like that. Tunnels are important, apparently...

They have gone.

16.

Linda's letter.

Linda You'll never guess what, Marigold. That girl from the shop you worked in. Jane, I think she's called. She's the new management trainee. They must be hard up. And to think that's what you were being offered. You could've done that standing on your head. But you didn't enjoy working there - I knew that. You only did it to keep your dad happy, didn't you. *(pause)* I wonder if he's happy now. *(pause)* No, I didn't mean that.

Silence.

Did you ever get to talk to him about... you know, the future? I don't suppose so. He'll never know what you really wanted, will he? Maybe he didn't want to.

Silence.

Did I tell you the play's been cancelled? It didn't seem - right, somehow, carrying on without... without Lady Macbeth. Well, you can't do a play with one of the main characters missing, can you? Poor old Macbeth would've had no one to talk to. Except himself, of course. He does a lot of that. *(pause)* I think I'll be doing a lot of that too, now. Oh Marigold, it's so difficult.. It's going to be so difficult.

17.

Linda has called for Marigold. Andrea is home from work.

Linda You mean she hasn't told you about it?

Andrea Marigold and I don't have much in common. She could tell me if she wanted.

Linda She's so excited about getting the part I thought you'd all be the first to know.

Andrea Yes, well, I'm not interested in that sort of thing. I have to earn a living, you know. I haven't got time for prancing about in plays or giving myself airs about going to university.

Linda I bet you could've gone if you'd wanted. Marigold says you're the really bright one in the family.

Andrea She said that? She's so modest, isn't she? Well, I was bright enough to take my father's advice and go out to work as soon as I could.

Linda Don't you sometimes wonder what you might have missed?

Andrea No. Why should I?

Linda No reason, I suppose. It's just that Marigold is so excited about the way things are turning out for her - it seems strange you and she could be so different.

Andrea Yeah, well we only live in the same house by a quirk of fate. And not for much longer, hopefully.

Linda gives her a sort of sympathetic look.

Don't look at me like that, Linda. I'm doing all right.

Linda looks at her again. A door closes offstage.

Elizabeth *(offstage)* Oh, Marigold, there you are. Linda's waiting for you.

Andrea There she is. You can go off to your rehearsal now.

Linda starts to leave.

Linda I hope you'll come and see the play, Andrea. You might be quite surprised by your little sister. She looks up to you, you know.

Andrea Well, nobody's perfect - even Marigold. Anyway, like I said, I don't have time for plays - *(with a hint of regret)* I'm always too tired.

Linda Yes. *(pause)* I'd better go. 'Bye.

She exits. Andrea does not respond.

18.

Graham and Elizabeth, together but not close to one another. A few moments' silence.

Elizabeth You might at least try to take an interest in what the children are doing.
Graham *(grudgingly)* I do take an interest.
Elizabeth There's precious little sign of it. When was the last time you spoke to Andrea about her job, or Marigold about this play she's auditioning for, or Simon about his schoolwork? They think you don't care.
Graham I don't get much chance, do I? You know I'm not home very often.
Elizabeth Yes, Graham. I certainly do know that. You might make more of an effort when you *are* here, that's all.
Graham Well, I'm here now, aren't I? Where are they all? They're not exactly queuing up to seek my advice are they? *(pause)* I do the best I can, Elizabeth. I've had to make my own way. I didn't have any of the advantages you seem to think our kids should have. I didn't get any of the choices they seem to take for granted. Well, it's a big, nasty world and they'll have to fend for themselves. *(pause)* And I can't for the life of me see how being in a play or going to university will make it any easier for them. You should see some of the people who work with me, the ones with degrees. They're no better off than the rest of us who left school when we were told and went out and worked for a living, instead of sponging off the taxpayer for three years. And then what? Some wonderful job at the end of it? Forget it! You get what you deserve in this life, and what you deserve is what you work for.

Silence.

Elizabeth Does that include your children?
Graham What do you mean by that?
Elizabeth Oh, nothing. Just one day you might turn round and find it's too late.
Graham Don't get clever with me, Elizabeth. *(pause)* If the children want to talk over anything with me, they know where to find me.
Elizabeth Do they, Graham? Do they?

19.

School. Simon is sitting alone. Miss Traynor approaches him.

Miss Traynor Hello, Simon. Not your usual irrepressible self today?
Simon I was just thinking.
Miss Traynor Thinking, eh? Dangerous pastime for a young man of your age. Who knows what might come of it?
Simon Well, I can't help it, Miss. Dangerous or not.

A short silence.

Miss Traynor You're late leaving today, aren't you?
Simon I don't feel like going home yet.
Miss Traynor Sounds pretty serious. Most of your peers can't wait to get out the gates. *(ruminatively)* Not that that means they're all rushing off home, of course.
Simon Will Marigold get a part in the play, Miss?
Miss Traynor Well, Simon, the auditions aren't until next week, and I always keep an open mind when it comes to casting. *(pause)* But I would certainly be disappointed if your sister doesn't audition for a part. She's very talented, I think. Not just in drama - in all sorts of ways. I think she has a very exciting future.
Simon I wish you could tell my Mum and Dad that - especially Dad. The only future he understands for any of us is the one that's the same as his past.

Pause.

Miss Traynor How's Andrea getting on? I always felt she would do well for herself.
Simon Andrea is the empirical proof that the Simon Simmons Theory of Future Expectations is right. She's in a job I know she's going to end up hating, because she expected to be; and she expected to be because she feels she wasn't given a choice. Probably she wasn't. And eventually she'll blame it all on the rest of us 'specially Marigold.
Miss Traynor Well, Simon. I know family conflicts can be difficult to deal with. But I think Marigold knows - and I hope you will too in a couple of years' time - that in the end you have to follow your own instincts. I'm sure that's what Marigold will do. I hope you do too.
Simon *(getting up)* It's easy for you to say that, Miss. I bet you had it easy.
Miss Traynor Well, I hope for your sake that you're not a gambling man, Simon.
Simon I'd better go. Back to the House of Doom!
Miss Traynor You'll be all right, Simon, as long as you keep your sense of humour. There's a funny side to everything. You'll see.

20.

Linda's letter.

Linda I don't know what else to say, Marigold. I bet you know what I'm thinking, anyway. You always seemed to when you were... *(pause)* What are *you*, thinking, I wonder. How unfair it all is, perhaps. That's what it seems to me, anyway. Why should someone like you end up as just another statistic? Why couldn't it have been someone else? *(pause)* But then you have to think about who the someone else might be, don't you? Why does it have to be anyone at all? Because then there wouldn't be any statistics, I suppose. And of course you must always have statistics in a well-ordered society. *(pause)* And if you're going to be a statistic, why does it have to be at the wrong time? When so many things are left unfinished, unspoken... when it's too late. *(pause)* And what am I going to do now? That's what I'd like to know. And how can I be so selfish as even to think a thing like that? We each have our own private feelings, don't we? Things we don't mind admitting to ourselves. We wouldn't like anyone else to know what they are, though, would we?

Silence.

So I suppose this is goodbye.

Pause.

It's such a final word, isn't it? Goodbye. Although we never realise that until goodbye really means goodbye.

Pause

Do we, Marigold?

21.

Each character inhabits his or her own space on the stage. Lines in square brackets are spoken simultaneously.

Simon I'm going to miss you so much, Marigold. I could always talk to you. I just wish Mum and Dad could have known you as well as I did, Marigold. Now they'll [never have the chance to/

Andrea Never have the chance to] tell you what I really felt, Marigold, even though I always meant to. I know I always seemed indifferent to what you were doing. Simon thinks it was just jealousy. Maybe he's right. [I don't know/

Elizabeth I don't know] if I ever told you - really - that I hoped you'd go to university, Marigold. Your father was always so... set in his ideas. Perhaps I should have been stronger, stood up to him more. But [I'm tired/

Graham I'm tired] of people telling me how I ought to deal with my own family. People think I'm narrow-minded, I daresay, but it hasn't done me any harm, and I was always ready to give you good advice, Marigold, if only you'd been prepared to [listen to me/

Vicky Listen to me] someone. I was her friend, wasn't I? I knew her pretty well. And I know she was better than me at all sorts of things - not just acting. But at least [she was my friend/

Linda She was my friend.] I'm going to [miss her/

Jane Miss her?] Well, I suppose we'll have to get someone else in the shop, [now she's gone/

Miss Traynor Now she's gone] and we must try to get on with things as best we can. Of course there'll always be a gap - but time will lessen it. I had such high hopes for her. Perhaps I shouldn't have had - but you can't help it with [someone like Marigold/

Andrea Someone like Marigold] - you don't realise who she is until [she's not
there any more/

Vicky She's not there any more] now, so I'll just have to find another friend. [I
don't know how/

Elizabeth I don't know how] we're going to get through [the next few months/

Graham The next few months] are bound to be difficult for all of us. But if you want
to know [what I think/

Jane What I think] is Mr Porter will make me permanent assistant manager
[before long/

Vicky Before long] people will be saying [Marigold who?/

Simon Marigold who?] I'll tell you who. My sister.

Elizabeth Daughter.

Andrea Sister.

Graham Daughter.

Miss Traynor Pupil.

Vicky Friend.

Jane Workmate.

The sequence gradually speeds up.

Simon Sister.

Elizabeth Daughter.

Andrea Sister.

Graham Daughter.

Miss Traynor Pupil.

Vicky Friend.

Jane Workmate.

Simon Sister.

Elizabeth Daughter.

Andrea Sister.

Graham Daughter.

Miss Traynor Pupil.

Vicky Friend.

Jane Workmate.

Simon Sister.

Elizabeth Daughter.

Andrea Sister.

Graham Daughter.

Miss Traynor Pupil.

Vicky Friend.

Jane Workmate.

Linda Friend! Marigold was my friend. My friend! *(pause)* You are my friend,
Marigold. Always. With love. Linda.

The lights fade slowly.

<u>Some other one-act plays available from Jaspers</u>

BEGINNERS and STICKERS
8F and 6F 1M. Two one-act plays in one volume.
Jane Witton
CARING and WHETHER DAMNED OR NOT
3F and 2M 2F. Two one-act plays in one volume.
Alan Crocker
EUROPEAN UNIONS and YOU JUST DON'T KNOW
2M 3F and 1M 3F. Two one-act plays in one volume.
Alan Crocker
GILLY'S GEM
4F 1M. HTV Award - 'Best original play.'
Sandy Taylor
GOSSIP
10F 2M. 'Best original play' Woking Drama Festival.
Robert Sheppard
GUESS WHO'S COMING TO TEA etc.,
9M 7F, 4M 5F and 2M 5F. Three award-winning plays in one volume.
Sandy Taylor
HOLIDAY SNAPS
5 'Theme related' plays in one volume. Small casts.
Jim Sperinck
HOLMES SWEET HOLMES
3M 3F. 'A Triumph' Edwin Parks, Journalist.
'A machine built to arouse laughter - extremely successful' Colin Pinney.
Jim Sperinck
INDEPENDENT'S DAY
3M 2F.
Mary Jackson
ONE DOWN THREE ACROSS
1M 3F. Winner 'South West Playwriting Competition.'
Mary Jackson
SNOW WHITE'S REVENGE
4F 2M.
Mary Jackson
TWO LITTLE DICKY BIRDS etc.,
2F 1M, 2F 1M and 3F. Three award-winning one-act plays.
Sandy Taylor

Jasper Publishing
1 Broad Street Hemel Hempstead Herts HP2 5BW
Tel: 01442 263461 Fax: 01442 217102